Contents

Sally Morgan

Hey there, Smart Girl

Wow, life, there's a big subject for you. Pretty important, lots to cover, best crack on and all that.

So, who am I to talk to you about life? Well, I like to think I am a Smart Girl now, but I haven't always felt that way. At primary school I was put in a group for children who struggled to learn to read and write. I HATED school a lot of the time. I was lazy and I was NEVER allowed to sit next to my friends because I talked way too much. I had my share of bad luck, too. My Dad died when I was six and that left me really sad for a long time. I did have great friends, but like a lot of you, I was bullied and, probably like some of you, I also bullied. Somehow, I realized I had to work hard and make better choices if I wanted things to change and because of that, I am writing this to you, sitting in a cosy coffee shop.

Right now, I am living the life I want. I make my living writing books and I love it! Not bad for a girl who struggled to learn to read and has dreadful handwriting. I had to work really hard and make a lot of tough choices to get here, but now I love where I am and know it was worth every minute. I am really proud of what I have achieved. #YayMe!

Life is going to happen to you whether you decide to take control or not, but living the life you want isn't about what you are given. Living the life you want is about making smart choices, working really hard and having a lot of fun along the way. Good luck!

Sally xxx

Smart Girl Rules

Life is all about making the right choices. Start following these rules today to make sure you lead the best life you can...

Today I choose to...

1. Never take feeling good or happy for granted.

2. Say 'yes' to life's opportunities.

3. Forgive myself when I mess up.

4. Stand up for what I believe in.

5. Remember that how I feel right now isn't how I'll feel forever.

6. Surround myself with good friends.

7. Be kind whenever I have the opportunity.

8. Make time for the things that are important to me.

9. Believe that I can achieve anything.

10. Learn to laugh at myself.

Take the Plunge: Revealing Quiz

Are you leading the life you want? Do you feel envious of people's lives around you? Well then, let's do something about it. Find out how you feel about your life with these six quick questions.

1. You hear that your school is having auditions for the play and you'd love to get a part in it. You…

a. Put your name on the list right away. This could be the start of your fabulous acting career.
b. Decide to wait until next time. You are already busy and don't want to overstretch yourself.
c. Don't bother. They always pick the same people so there is no point signing up.

2. You are on holiday and they have a kids' club at the resort. The kids in the club seem to be having a great time. You…

a. Ask your parents if you can join them. You have always wanted to try waterskiing.
b. Think about it. Maybe tomorrow, you've just started your magazine.
c. Stay well away. There's no way it will be as fun as it looks and what if no one talks to you?

3. You have a big test next week and you want to get a good mark. You…

a. Get studying!
b. Feel nervous so you spend all of your time making a beautiful study timetable.
c. It's hard and boring so you check if your favourite TV show is on to take your mind off it.

4. Your teacher says that the student with the best animal project will get the chance to help out at the local vets for the day. You love animals so you…

a. Put 100 per cent into your project. This is just your thing.
b. Imagine how much fun you'll have with the animals and not leave enough time for your project.
c. Do your project but try not to get too excited. There is no way it will be you.

5. A new girl starts at your school and your teacher asks for a volunteer to show her around. You...

a. Put your hand up – you are happy to help.
b. Wait to see if anyone else volunteers. You'd prefer to get to know her in your own time.
c. Keep your hands in your pockets and avoid eye contact with your teacher.

6. Your mum says that you can have a birthday party and invite anyone you like. You...

a. Immediately invite your whole class, your swimming club, the chess club and the school magazine. This is going to be the best party ever!
b. Plan an awesome party in your head but send the invites too late.
c. Only invite your best friend over for a sleepover. What if you invite other people and they don't come?

Conclusion

Mostly As – in at the deep end

You are always the first to sign up for everything. You love life and want to get as much out of it as possible. Make sure you don't take on too much though, you don't want to tire and stress yourself out.

Mostly Bs – paddling in the shallow end

You have big dreams and can't wait to start living them … tomorrow. It is a good idea to think before you leap but make sure your chances don't pass you by. Life is short, so get organized, get involved and start having fun!

Mostly Cs – still in the changing room

It's not that you don't have ambitions, it's just that you get nervous and don't want to be disappointed. Try to put your nerves to one side, put on your favourite outfit, pretend you are feeling confident and get out there.

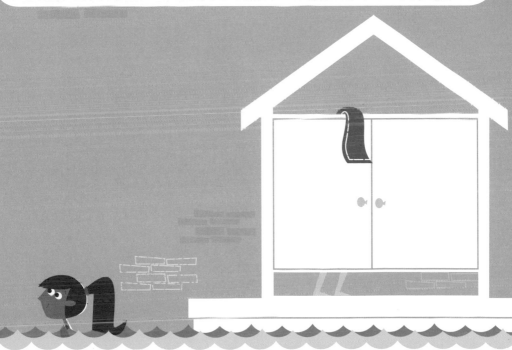

Life's Obstacle Course

You

There are so many things you want to do with your life, and some things you need to do, but sometimes things get in your way. Follow these Smart Girl tips to dealing with them.

Procrastination

Ever put off doing things until later? Like finding out Zayn Malik's favourite colour, rather than starting a new project? Stay alert for procrastination and remember, the sooner you finish your project, the sooner you can get back to doing what you want without feeling guilty about it or being nagged. #JustDoIt!

Disorganization

Do you ever have so much to do that it really stresses you out? Well, make a list of all the things you have to do, then give each one a mark from one to ten, with one being least important and ten being most. Cross off anything on the list that is below a five and leave it for another day.

Fear of failing

Do you get scared of trying new things? Well don't let that stop you, a lot of scary things can be exciting. Imagine yourself succeeding, or think about what it is you're scared of. So what if you find out you aren't a natural ballet dancer or realize you hate surfing? Simply try something else. At least you'll have a funny story to tell afterwards.

Negative Nellies

Do some of your friends love to dampen your good mood? Ugh! These are the worst dream crushers known to Smart-Girlkind. They like to claim they are being 'realistic'. Tackle these damsels of doom with a nod and smile and ignore everything they say. Keep on smiling and prove them wrong. They'll never admit it and that is why it's rubbish to be them.

Class Act

'Kids at school nicknamed me "alien" and they threw rocks at me.' Jessie J

'I didn't fit in in high school, and I felt like a freak.' Lady Gaga

The best days of your life? LOL
Five reasons why school sucks…

1. Uniforms If you have one you'll know how hard it is to rock the shapeless-jumper-and-pleated-skirt look. Ugh!

2. Lunch Whether it's soggy sandwiches or school dinners from the cafeteria, when you are a grown-up there is no way you'll eat like this.

3. Teachers Some are just okay but the rest you doubt are even human. There is no way they were ever young … ever.

4. Mornings Why does school have to start so early? Don't grown-ups realize that you would do so much better if it could start at 11 o'clock?

5. PE You're all for keeping fit, but running around the school hall with a beanbag on your head is just humiliating. Yoga anyone?

The best days of your life? Maybe

Five reasons why school rocks...

1. Friends

It might not be your first choice of venue, but at least you get to see your friends and catch up on the latest gossip.

2. Lunch

The food may be awful but a whole hour to hang out with your favourite gal pals is awesome.

3. PE

Okay, so running around the school hall with a beanbag on your head can be hilarious if you are with the right people and at least it's not assembly ... right?

4. After-school clubs

Whether it is the drama club, the rounders team or chess, there are so many fun things to choose from you don't know where to start.

5. Holidays

Christmas, Easter, half term ... the summer ... ahhh! You are rarely more than six weeks away from your next break. Smile – the term will be over before you know it.

Learning to speak 'Teacher'

Ever feel like your teacher is speaking a foreign language even when you are studying English? Read on to become fluent in the mysterious language of 'Teacherspeak'.

'See me'

It can be scary when you see this written in red pen on your homework, but don't panic. Teachers have A LOT of books to mark and don't have time to write an explanation on everyone's work. They probably just want to help you understand something a bit better. You are at school to learn, so listen up.

'Could do better'

Feel sad that your teacher doesn't think you are trying hard enough? Stop that now. 'Could do better' means your teacher sees great things in you and wants to see you achieve them. If you're struggling, why not ask them to give you a few pointers. They will be pleased to see you making the effort.

There are no stupid questions

If you ask, 'Did people love Justin Bieber in the Middle Ages?', you will soon discover that this statement isn't entirely true. Your teacher wants you to feel like you can ask them anything, but they would prefer it if you stayed on topic.

There are no wrong answers

When a teacher says this they want you to think creatively and be brave. So what if you say something silly – you never know, things might just get interesting ... for a change.

Teacher Terror

Are there times that you feel that you can't do anything right? When you are 100 per cent sure that your teacher hates you and has it in for you? Read on to tackle teacher terror head on and come out smiling on the other side.

Getting them to like you

Hmm … with real terrors this might not be possible. Any attempt to suck up to them or win them over could be seen as a bit creepy. Instead of trying to get them to like you, aim to get them to ignore you. Get your work done as well as you can and avoid drawing any unnecessary attention to yourself. He or she won't be your teacher forever so you'll soon have your chance to shine.

Everything you do drives them crazy

Watch your teacher carefully, all teachers have their touch points that make them lose their cool – does she flip out when people are giggling or talking when she is talking? Or does late and messy homework make her go crazy? When you have worked out what her buttons are, do your best not to push them.

Suck it up, sister

Perhaps this teacher is just plain odd. It happens and it is really bad luck. As you grow up you are going to meet people that you don't get along with – no matter what you do, they just seem to be immune to your fabulousness. Try to remember at all times that you rock, no matter what they think. You are better than them so rise above it, be polite and remember they will not be in your life forever.

Talk about it

Talk to your friends and an adult you trust. Some of their advice may be dreadful, but talking about it will make you feel less alone. Also, if your teacher really is a problem, an adult you trust may be able to speak to them or the school on your behalf.

Get Organized to De-stress

Sometimes school stress can be overwhelming. Between homework, chores, after-school clubs, walking the dog, looking after your little brother and trying to fit in as much reality TV as possible there aren't enough hours in the day! Eliminate school stress and get organized with these worry-busting tips.

GET UP!

If you struggle to get up in the morning, set your alarm one hour before you need to leave the house. This will give you plenty of time to snooze, wash, dress, have breakfast and double check that you have everything you need.

GET IN!

Unpack your school bag and change into your house clothes as soon as you get in. Give your parents any notes from school and anything that needs washing. You will be able to de-stress much quicker if you know all of this is taken care of.

GET ORGANIZED!

If you know you've got hockey on Monday, it's the next episode of your favourite show on Wednesday and you're going away for the whole weekend, then don't procrastinate. Get your homework done on Tuesday and Thursday for a guilt-free week. Simple!

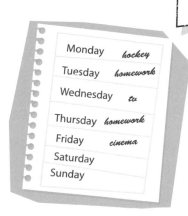

Monday	*hockey*
Tuesday	*homework*
Wednesday	*tv*
Thursday	*homework*
Friday	*cinema*
Saturday	
Sunday	

GET IT DONE!

Make a space to do your homework and get it done ASAP. This will give you the rest of the night off and stop that 9 o'clock panic when you remember the homework you haven't done. When you've finished, put it straight back in your bag so you don't forget it in the morning.

GET TO BED!

Pack your school bag before you go to bed. Make sure you have your homework, your PE kit if you need it and any notes that you needed your parents to sign. You will sleep much better knowing that you are prepared for the next day. Sleep is also an excellent stress buster and improves your memory, so make sure you are getting enough, about 10 hours a night.

Agony Aunt

Your school troubles sorted…

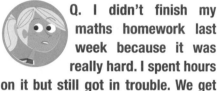

Q. I didn't finish my maths homework last week because it was really hard. I spent hours on it but still got in trouble. We get maths homework every week, it's so unfair! What should I do?

A. Unfortunately, you can't get out of maths homework, but you can make this situation easier. Speak to your teacher. Show him or her your homework after class and tell them how long you spent on it. Explain which bits you found hard. Don't worry about feeling stupid, you are at school to learn and it's smart to ask for help. When your teacher understands, he or she will give you the extra help you need. Honestly it'll make things easier in the long run.

Q. I am frightened of the big kids at my new school. At my last school, I was in one of the oldest classes and I knew everyone. What should I do?

A. Poor little fish! Moving from being a big fish in a little pond to being a tiny fish in an enormous ocean can feel really scary. Try joining a lunchtime or after-school club that has students from different years. As soon as you get to know some of the big kids, you'll see that they are just like you, but bigger, and not so scary after all.

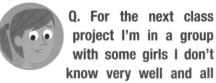

Q. For the next class project I'm in a group with some girls I don't know very well and all my friends are together. I feel left out and sad. Should I ask to switch?

A. You could ask to switch, but don't be surprised if your teacher says, 'no' #SoUnfair! Use this opportunity to get to know some other people in your class a bit better. You might find you work better without your best buds to chat to. This project won't last forever and your friends will be sure to fill you in on anything you missed out on.

Q. I hate school. I dread going so much that I feel sick every morning. My teacher is nice and I have friends but I hate going. How can I persuade my Mum to stop making me go?

A. You might have 'school phobia', where a person is so scared of going to school that they have real physical symptoms, like feeling and being sick, headaches and sleeplessness. Talk to a grown-up you trust about how you feel. They can make an appointment at school to discuss what it is you are scared of and what can be done to make it easier for you. The most important thing is that you speak to someone about it. The sooner you speak to someone, the sooner you can start feeling better.

Q. I am being teased at school because I get good marks and put my hand up to answer questions. I like school but I don't like getting picked on. What should I do?

A. Yay for you! You're a Smart Girl that's going places, but it can be hard to remember that when you are being called names. Whatever you do, don't dumb yourself down. Some people find schoolwork hard, and rather than studying, they like to tease others to distract from themselves. If you really can't take the heat, maybe keep your hand down for a couple of days until the dust settles. Just remember, you are SMART and that's AWESOME!

When School Really, Really Sucks...

Let's face it, school can be really tough sometimes. Not all the girls you meet are going to be gal pals for life; some of them are just plain evil. You might feel that no one there 'gets' you. Teachers can be difficult. You aren't likely to ace every test you take. After-school clubs?! Ha, you don't go to those because you would prefer to spend as little time in the place as possible. Sometimes school can feel like the WORST place on the planet.

Everybody feels like this sometimes, and some people feel like this all the time but there is one thing you must remember: SCHOOL DAYS ARE NOT FOREVER. Even if everything goes wrong at school, you have no friends and you do dreadfully in all of your classes WHO YOU ARE AT SCHOOL IS NOT WHO YOU ARE FOREVER. So keep your head down, take a breath and find things outside of school to help pass the time. Focus on all of the fabulous people who also had a tough time at school and how things got better for them. You can't guarantee many things about your school days except that some of them will be totally dull and they will eventually end.

Successful women who hated school:

'I was bullied when I was 12 years old. I'm not saying I was totally innocent – I had my bratty days!' Demi Lovato

Lady Gaga

Christina Aguilera

Hilary Swank

'What I've noticed is that almost no one who was a big star in high school is also big star later in life. For us overlooked kids, it's so wonderfully fair.' Mindy Kaling

Megan Fox

Victoria Beckham

'I was bullied every second of every day in elementary and middle school.' Selena Gomez

Kate Winslet

Sandra Bullock

'I'd eat my lunch in the nurses' office so I didn't have to sit with the other girls.' Jessica Alba

Jennifer Garner

Rihanna

Zooey Deschanel

Jessie J

Home
Life

'I think sometimes when children grow up, their parents grow up... Mine grew up with me. We coexist. I don't try to change them anymore, and I don't think they try to change me.' Katy Perry

'I always say Mum is my absolute hero and I mean it. I couldn't survive without her. She's sacrificed so much not just for me but for my two sisters as well' – Rebecca Adlington

When navigating the world of parents, even a Smart Girl could use a little help. Parents are funny creatures, some days they can be your best friends, having fun and being silly. They are great when you are sick or feeling sad and even though they can sometimes be a little embarrassing, you wouldn't be without them for all the cupcakes in the world. Other days they are very different. Parents can be VERY embarrassing in front of your friends and seem to exist only to stop you living the life you want. These are the days that you know that they were never your age, or if they were they were some kind of freak who obeyed all the rules and ate lunch with the teachers. Why would you want to behave the way they want if it means you might turn out like them? Like really?! ARRRRGH! They are SO annoying. Read on for help with these weird creatures.

Decoding
Parent Speak

'We'll see...'

Ugh! This is very annoying and one of the more irritating parental 'go-to' phrases. Even more annoyingly, if you ask the parent what 'we'll see' actually means it is usually followed pretty quickly with a more forceful, 'I SAID, WE'LL SEE!' What your parent is trying to do is to buy himself or herself some time. They may have already decided on the answer to whatever it was that you asked them, or they may not. One thing they have decided on is that now is not the time to discuss it. Your best move is to hedge your bets, they may not have decided that the answer is 'no' ... yet. You do not want to force them into it. Bide your time and wait until you think your parent may be having a 'Golden Moment' (see page 35) and ask again. You never know, you may be able to turn this 'we'll see' into a 'yes!'

'When I was your age...'

Parents love pretending that it was less than a gazillion years since they were your age. What's really annoying is that this is usually the beginning of a lecture on how hard they had it and how lucky you are. Yawn!

'When I was your age we didn't have the Internet to do our homework. We had to go to the library and if there were no books left we would fail ... yadda ... yadda ... yadda...'

Be kind, it isn't their fault, they really don't know they are ancient.

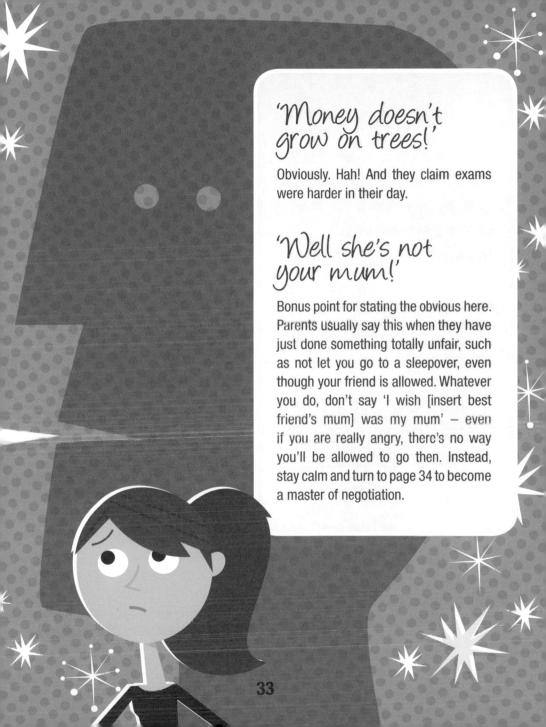

'Money doesn't grow on trees!'

Obviously. Hah! And they claim exams were harder in their day.

'Well she's not your mum!'

Bonus point for stating the obvious here. Parents usually say this when they have just done something totally unfair, such as not let you go to a sleepover, even though your friend is allowed. Whatever you do, don't say 'I wish [insert best friend's mum] was my mum' – even if you are really angry, there's no way you'll be allowed to go then. Instead, stay calm and turn to page 34 to become a master of negotiation.

Negotiation Skills

Being good at negotiating isn't just about getting what you want, but it helps. Negotiating is about achieving an outcome that is good for everyone… Maybe you want a new phone, or your life won't be complete unless you go to your best friend's sleepover. Follow these Smart Girl tips to make sure your parents see your point of view.

Choosing your moment

When asking for the impossible, timing is everything. Be patient and wait. Don't keep asking when you're mad, it gets you nowhere and just makes your parents more annoyed. Also, avoid times of stress. You're never going to get a good response when your parents are trying to get everyone out of the door for swimming or elbow deep in a gory 'gift' from the cat – eww! If you are unsure if your parent is stressed, use this Smart Girl checklist.

- **Red or sweating face**
- **excessive use of sarcasm**
- **the use, or almost use, of BAD words**
- **gritted teeth**
- **throbbing veins in the head or neck.**

You wouldn't approach a lion, a tiger or even a honey badger (look it up) that was behaving like this and parents, under stress, should be treated like any other wild animal.

- Take a step back
- be cooperative and offer to help
- stay quiet
- smile – without bearing your teeth, a parent could take this for a snarl.

The Golden Moment

Your parents will be much more likely to say 'yes' if they are relaxed. This is a Golden Moment – use it wisely. To identify whether or not your parent may be experiencing a Golden Moment see the checklist below.

- Shoulders are down
- silly warm smile
- they have just eaten something nice
- they have a glass of their favourite drink in their hands
- your grandparents have just left.

How to present your case

Do your research – have all available data at your fingertips.

- How much will it cost?
- how long will it take?
- will parents be there?
- how will it benefit them?*

- what are the alternatives?
- what are the pros and cons?
- what have you honestly done to deserve it?

* When entering into a negotiation it is important to remember that everyone wants to leave the table feeling like they are getting a good deal.

Follow these Smart Girl rules and you might just find that you're starting to hear 'yes' a lot more than 'no'. If you're really good, maybe you should consider a career as a lawyer – they argue for a living!

Agony Aunt

Your parental problems pulverized...

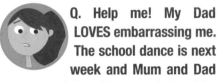

Q. Help me! My Dad LOVES embarrassing me. The school dance is next week and Mum and Dad are supervising. How can I stop him from making me look silly?

A. You are suffering from 'embarrassing parentitus' and I am afraid there is no cure. With most parental problems a Smart Girl can sit the offending parent down and tell them exactly how they are making her feel. This WILL NOT work it will only make matters worse. Those feelings of shame, social terror and rage are exactly how your Dad wants you to feel. Why is a mystery. Ignoring his behaviour could also backfire and make him worse. Try talking to your Mum, maybe she can keep an eye on him. The only other option is to embrace his behaviour and rise above it. He's your Dad, make sure everybody knows it, don't pretend you aren't with him. Instead use him to make yourself look cool and sophisticated in comparison to his wrinkled buffoonery. He might think he is the big man, but you can be the bigger person.

Q. My little sister is SO annoying. She is younger than me, but she doesn't seem to know it. She sneaks into my room and breaks my stuff, then I get told off. How can I make her go away and leave me alone?

A. On TV you are led to believe that a sister can be your BFF but you know better. Sisters steal your things and get you into trouble all the time. They can be really irritating, but they can have their uses. Ask yourself why your sister wants to mess with your things? Is it because they are way cooler than all of her babyish toys? To stop her messing with your stuff, try complimenting some of her belongings. Make her feel good about her room and it will make yours much less interesting to her. Invite her into your room when you need to tidy it, you might even be able to get her to help you. While she is there, give her some of the things you don't use any more. This act of sisterly kindness should help take the mystery out of your room. Good luck!

 Q. I REALLY want a new bike. My old one is bright pink and lame. I asked for a new one for my birthday but my parents say they can't afford it. What should I do?

 A. Let's not bother with the whole you-are-very lucky-to-even-have-a-bike argument. You know that, you feel bad about that, but you still want a new bike, right? Well, first of all, stop nagging, stop whining and leave it for a while. If your parents have told you that they don't have enough money, banging on and on about it will only either make them angry or feel bad, and it doesn't just make the money appear. Do some research. So there isn't enough money for a new bike, perhaps there might be enough for a new-to-you bike? Have a look online, try ebay.co.uk and gumtree.com. Make a note of how much one you like costs and bring it up with your parents again. They might not say 'yes' right away, but you'll have shown you understand and are being mature about it. This will make them think about the bike thing again. Fingers crossed you will be pedalling away on a new-to-you set of wheels before you know it.

Remember: NEVER give out any personal details to ANYONE online and NEVER agree to meet anyone or arrange a sale without asking your parents' permission first.

#SGG
to Living
Online

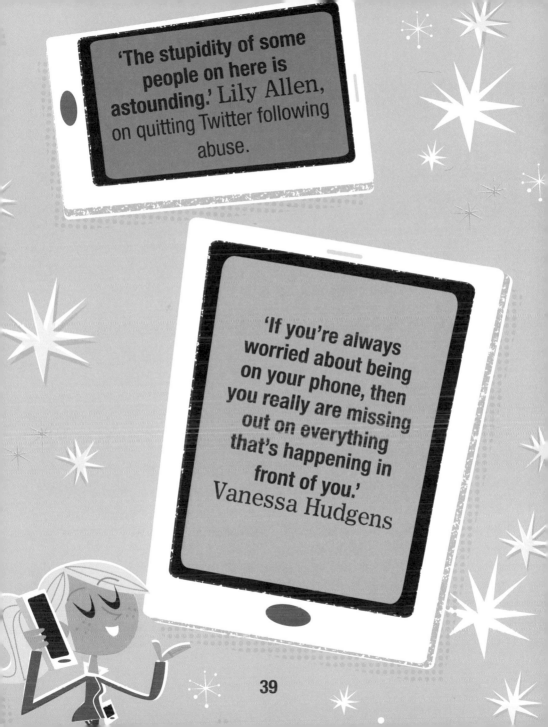

'The stupidity of some people on here is astounding.' Lily Allen, on quitting Twitter following abuse.

'If you're always worried about being on your phone, then you really are missing out on everything that's happening in front of you.' Vanessa Hudgens

39

Cyber-life Smart

With so much of a Smart Girl's life happening online, it can be very easy to get carried away with too many personal posts and selfies.

Follow these simple Smart Girl tips to make sure you stay safe and happy. There are strange people on the Internet so be careful.

1. Don't sign up to any sites, especially social networking sites, without asking your parents first - okay, big snore, but this is really important.

2. Many sites have age restrictions that are designed to keep you safe. Make sure you obey them.

3. Don't post any photos or videos without checking with your parents first.

4. NEVER agree to meet anyone you have met online - sometimes people aren't what they seem. If somebody asks you to meet up, stop messaging that person immediately and tell your parents or a teacher.

5. Never give your last name, phone number, address or school name. Just because a person or a website asks you for information doesn't mean you have to give it.

6. Don't believe everything you read on the Internet!

7. Don't open any attachments, even from people you know, without checking with your parents first. Attachments can contain viruses that can break your computer or even spy on you.

•••• VERY IMPORTANT SMART GIRL RULE ••••

People can behave very differently online to how they would if they were talking to you face to face. If anyone says anything that makes you uncomfortable or you find anything written about you that upsets you, tell an adult you trust immediately. They can find out who posted it and have it taken down. People can get in a lot of trouble for posting unkind things about others.

Don't say anything to or about someone online that you wouldn't say to his or her face. In fact if you haven't got anything nice to say, don't say anything at all. No one likes trolls, so stop before you post and think. Don't be one, and don't let them get to you because, basically, they're idiots!

Be Your Own Publicist

O nline, image is everything. All celebrities have their own publicists to manage their online personas. Follow these Smart Girl tips to be your own and give yourself a profile even a professional would be proud of.

Choose an awesome login name

Get creative, why not choose the name of a favourite character from a book or TV show? Mix your name with a celebrity's or make up a cool new word. It looks way cooler than Chloe80609883.

Choose a photograph

Make sure you are smiling and looking like you are having fun. Some people think looking miserable looks cool. #SnoozeFest. Check the photo with your parents first. If they aren't happy for you to use a picture of yourself, choose a picture that says something about you, maybe a band you love, your favourite animal or a pair of shoes you'd love to own. #Louboutins

Keep it private

Adjust your privacy settings so that only you, your friends and family can see what you post to the site. This not only makes your posts exclusive to a select few, but also means that if you slip up or post anything embarrassing only your good friends can see it.

Google yourself

This is a great way to find out if anyone is talking about you online and has the added bonus of helping you to find out if there are any famous people with the same name as you. Remember to tell your parents if you find anything about yourself that makes you feel uncomfortable.

Don't be a bore

If you have just eaten the best ice-cream sundae EVER, sure, post it, but nobody wants to know what you have for breakfast every day.

Don't over share

How you feel that minute might not be how you feel in the morning and you've just

shared it with the whole world. Social media is for fun. Talk to family and friends if you're upset.

Keep it current

If it is more than a month old, take it down. Your profile is about who you are right now, not a diary about who you were a month ago. If the site won't let you remove old pictures and posts, consider changing sites – it's your information and you should be in charge of it.

The Tough Stuff

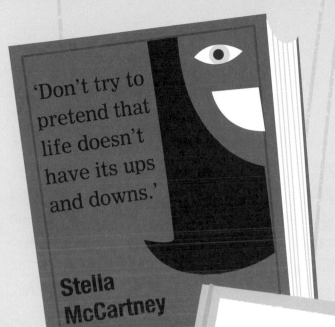

'Don't try to pretend that life doesn't have its ups and downs.'

Stella McCartney

'You don't change how sensitive you are. You just concentrate on other things; you allow the feelings to come in and to go. You find strength in your crazy parts.'

P!nk

How to Feel Smart

Sometimes it's easy to think that life would be much simpler if we didn't have feelings, but it is good to remember that for every difficult feeling, such as sadness, frustration, anger or resentment there is an easy, fun feeling such as happiness, satisfaction, peace and gratitude. Feeling Smart is all about figuring out exactly how you feel and what you can do to change it if you need to. Follow the simple steps below to figure out how to Feel Smart in any situation.

Keep a diary of how you are feeling

Keep a journal about what happened during your day and write down how it made you feel.

Laughed and then snot-bubbled in front of half of Year 6 – I was SO embarrassed! #TheHorror

Writing about your day will help you identify how you are feeling and give you a record of how you felt in the past. Sometimes things that made you feel really sad a few weeks ago can seem stupid to you when you look back at them.

Talk to someone you trust

Okay, so a problem shared isn't a problem halved, I mean, who would be able to work that out accurately anyway? A problem is still a problem whether you talk about it or not, but talking about it will give you another person's point of view on how you feel and they can help you work out what it is that is making you feel that way. Also, with the big stuff, talking to an adult you trust really can help to make that problem go away. Don't struggle with your feelings alone.

DO NOT take the easy way out

Try to be honest about why you feel the way you do, whenever you can. It is too easy to take your feelings out on other people and say things like – 'I HATE Alana, she thinks she is *soo* good, just because she got a "Very Good!" on her science homework … again. I think she cheats, I bet her brother did it for her, while she was getting that stupid new haircut.'

This is when a Smart Girl needs to take herself and her feelings in hand and Feel Smart. Ask yourself…

Do you really HATE Alana? Or are you just FRUSTRATED and JEALOUS that you got yet another low mark and 'See me'? Do you really think she cheats? Or do you just wish you knew how to do your homework as well as her?

47

What can you do about feeling so frustrated? Perhaps you could ask your teacher to give you a few extra pointers or even better why don't you ask Alana?

And the 'stupid new haircut' thing? Smart Girl – shame on you! This kind of spiteful lashing out comes from not Feeling Smart and being honest with yourself about why you feel the way you do. Saying something nasty can give you a little naughty thrill that can make you feel better, temporarily, but it will usually make you feel much worse in the long run. Being mean to someone

doesn't make you a better person. By working through your feelings, you stand a chance of understanding them and doing something about them.

Try to remember that if someone says something spiteful about you, it usually says far more about them.

Listen to others
Nobody likes to sit there while someone drones on about every minuscule non-

problem in their life – er, how about handing the mic over once in a while, Moaning Myrtle?! – but listening to other people talk about how they feel not only gives you the opportunity to be a good friend, but also helps you to keep your own problems in perspective. It can sometimes make you realize how lucky you are. At the very least, seeing how someone else handles their feelings can help you learn a lot about how to handle your own.

BEWARE!

If you find that listening to a particular friend leaves you feeling more unhappy, beware, there's nothing misery loves more than company. Be a good friend to her, but make sure you surround yourself with chicas of a more cheery persuasion too.

Difficult Feelings

There are no such things as good feelings or bad feelings. All feelings are natural, even though some of them make us feel dreadful. When you feel something difficult, like anger or stress, it is the same as when you feel pain, it means that there is something amiss. Read on for a few tips to some of life's more difficult feelings.

ANGER

Unfairness, teasing, failing, rules and parents are just a few of the things in life that might make you angry. There is nothing wrong with being angry, it can even be good to help motivate you to do better. But the problem with anger is when you don't recognize it, you lose control and say nasty things or become violent.

Anger can make you:
- **red faced and sweaty**
- **say horrible things**
- **cry**
- **violent**
- **get headaches and stomach aches.**

Try handling your anger before doing something you regret with these temper-taming tips:

- **breathe deeply and count to ten**
- **walk away**
- **exercise to burn off angry energy**
- **think of happy memories or something funny**
- **talk to someone**
- **sing at the top of your lungs.**

When you have calmed down, think about what it was that made you angry and why, and who you should speak to about it.

SADNESS

Like anger, lots of things in life will make you sad – not getting picked for a team, losing something important to you, someone moving away, falling out with friends, even someone else being sad can make you feel blue. It is natural for some things to make you feel sad but be careful it doesn't take over all areas of your life.

Sadness can make you:
- **clam up and not want to talk**
- **cry**
- **not want to get up in the morning**
- **stomp around grumpily**
- **angry**
- **misbehave.**

The next time you feel blue try some of these sadness-solving solutions:

- **talk to someone**
- **think positive and smile**
- **don't dwell, move on**
- **remember this feeling will pass**
- **treat yourself.**

Sadness is like a scab, sitting around and picking at it all day will only make it worse. Feeling positive and moving forward by treating yourself or being kind to others can make you feel much better. Most sadness will pass pretty quickly, but if you start to feel sad more often than happy it is very important that you talk to an adult you trust. Struggling on your own hasn't worked so far, so it is time to try something else.

51

NERVES

You are standing in front of the class about to read the poem you wrote and you freeze. Your hands feel sweaty, your stomach is churning, oh my goodness … you think you are going to cry. STOP! You're suffering from nerves.

Follow these four steps to move on from nervous to fabulous!

1. Focus on something still, like the clock or someone's painting of a silly owl, anything that isn't smiling or pulling faces.
2. Breathe in slowly through your nose and breathe out even more slowly through your mouth, whistling VERY QUIETLY through your teeth. Focus on the whistle. It is almost impossible to cry and whistle at the same time.
3. As you breathe, imagine yourself being filled with warm, glowing liquid confidence. Your hair looks great, everyone wants you to do well, even the owl picture. You were born to do this. Nothing is easier on this earth.
4. What are you standing there, breathing and whistling for? GO!

EMBARRASSMENT
#OhTheShame

The horror! You feel sweaty, flustered, your face is going red and you need to run, RUN far away! Enough to ruffle the feathers of even the smartest of girls, embarrassment is sneaky and cannot be predicted or prevented. It can cause anger, sadness, stress and make your cheeks burn! What can you do?

1. Check if anyone has noticed. If you don't draw attention to what happened, you might just get away with it. Fingers crossed.

2. Don't get hung up on what happened. Leave it where it belongs, in the past!

3. Laugh along if people tease you about it. If people think it bothers you they will bring it up even more.

4. Add a few jokes about it of your own. Come on … some things are just funny. ;)

5. If teasing bothers you, remember that this too shall pass. It may drive you crazy now, but it will be old news in no time.

6. Remember that what doesn't kill you makes you interesting. Embarrassing moments make great stories.

GUILT TRIP
#DestinationBetterYou

Ever done something so wrong that it left you feeling really horrible inside? Feeling guilty sucks, here's how to get through it and come out smiling on the other side.

Guilt can make you:
- **lose sleep and concentration**
- **cry**
- **feel really bad inside and judge yourself**
- **want to pretend as though you did nothing wrong.**

All this ickiness is hard work but it can be really good for you. Feeling guilty can also make you:

- **take responsibility**
- **do your best never to do it again**
- **remind you of how what you do affects others.**

Own up
Keeping guilt bottled up and not owning up will eat away at you. No matter how bad you think what you did was, you will feel better when you admit it and apologize. Even if you're not forgiven immediately, you've been honest and said 'sorry'.

Let it go
You did something, you felt bad, you said sorry – it's time to let it go. Constantly replaying the situation over and over is unhealthy. You've learnt from your mistake, you know better now and won't do it again, so stop punishing yourself.

Fake guilt begone!
Ever felt guilty when you know for a fact that you didn't do anything wrong? Like when your friend did really badly on a test and you did really well? This is fake guilt and won't help you or your friend. Let it go, you can still celebrate your success while supporting your friend through their difficult time.

STRESS

You will definitely have heard adults saying that they are stressed out, but what do they know about it … right? Between, school, friendships, homework, annoying siblings, after-school commitments and more homework, it's hard to keep on top of it all and stay calm.

A little stress can be really helpful. Good stress can make you feel just the right amount of nervous to make you get something done but too much stress is a bad thing.

When stress gets out of control, it can make you:
- **easily distracted and forgetful**
- **cry**
- **grumpy**
- **scared**
- **sleep badly**
- **eat differently**
- **have headaches and throw up.**

Follow these stress-stomping suggestions the next time you start to feel frazzled.

1. Write a list of what is stressing you out.
2. Take a deep breath and prioritize the important things.
3. Say 'no' to things you can't manage, you are a Smart Girl, not Super-Girl!
4. Talk about it.
5. Get some rest.
6. Eat plenty of fruit and veg rather than junk.

GOOD GRIEF

When you use lose someone you love the feeling of sadness that you experience is called grief.

Grief can make you:
- **angry with the person who died**
- **angry with people who aren't grieving the way you are**
- **angry with the people who haven't felt grief**
- **pretend that nothing has changed**
- **feel guilty about things you did or didn't say to the person that died**
- **lose sleep**
- **not want to eat**
- **feel numb and empty**
- **cry a lot right away and later, over unexpected things**
- **feel guilty every time you laugh or feel happy**
- **feel like you have to pretend to be happy to stop others feeling sad.**

Grief is different for everyone

When you grieve you may feel all of these things or none. Grief is different for everyone and just because someone doesn't cry or seems to carry on as normal, it doesn't mean that their grief is any less real than yours. Grief is a natural and very important emotion, and although it can be horrible it is the first step to feeling better.

Learn to share

Talking about your feelings can make you feel less alone, but it can be difficult. When you lose someone you love, it can be really hard to talk about them, even though you think about them all the time. Sometimes people around you are also grieving and that can make you not want to talk about the person that died in case you upset them. Take it slowly and only talk when you feel comfortable. Recall happy memories – remembering can be painful, but it can be comforting too.

Time heals, but not completely

When you lose someone or something it will be the biggest thing in your life for a long time. Eventually though, other parts of life will start sneaking in. This can make you feel guilty, but it shouldn't – your life has to, and should, go on. Your grief will never fully go away, you will always carry a little piece of it, but it will get easier and easier to handle.

57

Health

Menu

'We're always told what's beautiful and what's not, and that's not right.' Serena Williams

'What are you going to do? Be hungry every single day to make other people happy? That's just dumb.' Jennifer Lawrence

Get More Than Five a Day

You've probably heard how you are supposed to try to eat five pieces of fruit or veg a day, but did you know that some experts believe that you should eat eight?

Fruit and vegetables are full of vitamins and minerals to keep you healthy inside and out, fibre to keep your digestive system working and water to keep you hydrated. All that and they taste pretty good too! #Amazing! Follow these top tips to make sure you are getting enough of the good stuff.

Drink one – have a glass of fruit or vegetable juice to kick-start your day. Don't drink too much though – it's full of sugar and doesn't contain the fibre, which is one of the things that make fruit and vegetables so good for you.

Start early – eat some fruit for breakfast. Sprinkle some blueberries or raspberries onto your cereal or try sliced apple with your toast.

Snack smart – swap snacks for fruit. A fresh ripe nectarine or plum will keep your hunger pangs at bay much longer than a chocolate bar or bag of crisps.

Sneak them in – add peas or sweetcorn to your pasta sauce and add another vegetable to your evening meal. Meat and two veg? Make it meat and three.

Keep things interesting – experiment with different, new and exciting fruit and vegetables. Look out for exotic treats at the supermarket like kiwi fruit or dragon fruit.

Have dessert – chop up fresh fruit and serve with a dollop of Greek yoghurt and chopped nuts. #Yum!

What's on Your Plate?

There is no such thing as bad food, it's just all about moderation. Check out the too-good-to-be-true plate below to see how you should be eating each day. Try keeping these ratios in mind when you are making your packed lunch or choosing food in the school cafeteria.

Fruit and vegetables – make sure you are getting at least your five a day. See page 60.

Wholegrains and potatoes – switch from white to wholegrain bread and pasta whenever possible. It's packed with heart-healthy fibre.

Dairy – milk, yoghurt and cheese. Full of protein and calcium to keep your growing bones strong. Non-dairy alternatives include almond milk, nuts, green vegetables and soy.

Non-nutritional treats – you can have your favourite sugary drinks and sweets or anything very high in fat, like chips or doughnuts, just in moderation. Make sure that they don't make up too much of what you eat each day and enjoy the treat.

Non-dairy protein – lean meat, fish, beans. Proteins are the building blocks of every cell in your body so it makes sense that you need to eat some from time to time. They also help you feel full and so will stop you snacking.

Pictures of Health?

#PhotoFakes

Ever looked at a magazine, advert or poster and thought – 'I'd be so much happier if I looked like that'? Well stop. The people in the pictures probably feel the same way, but they are in on the secret – nobody really looks like that, not even them! Not so sure? Take a closer look.

Before

After

Skin

There are no freckles, no veins and DEFINITELY no spots. Can you even see any pores? This isn't skin. Real skin has freckles, veins, moles, hair, spots, scars and lots of pores. Models have REAL skin but theirs has been covered up with piles of make-up applied by experts. Any 'imperfection' is magically rubbed out on a computer screen, making their skin glossy and smooth.

Hair

Whether it's messy and shiny, or sleek and perfectly groomed, nobody wakes up in the morning with hair like this. Even the messy styles have taken experts months of training to achieve, and flyaway strands can be removed with more photo editing.

Eyes

Are they bright and shiny, with full lashes and no bags or lines? Not only are the eyelashes false but they're edited on the computer to look even thicker, and everything else has been rubbed away.

Teeth

They are always perfectly straight and whiter than white in pictures, but healthy teeth are supposed to be an off-white, creamy-yellow colour. Even if the model has had her teeth whitened, photo editors will still brighten them up.

Body

Is she tall, thin and bump free? Unless you are one of the very few who actually looks like this you'll know that real bodies don't resemble the ones in adverts. Even models' bodies are stretched, slimmed, toned and smoothed out to impossible shapes with editing software.

The Truth

Ever wondered why your magazines are mostly adverts? A lot of magazines aren't there to tell you things, they are there to sell you things. To do this, they need to make you feel just a little bit unhappy, that you wouldn't be completely happy until you owned those shoes or used that moisturizer or looked just like that model. Don't get sucked in – enjoy your magazine, but remember that none of it is real. Nobody really looks like that and nobody eats the perfect breakfast, got the perfect skin from a face wash, does 30 minutes of yoga before school, gets straight As and is perfectly hydrated, while being best friends with all of 1D. Nobody. Remember that and you will be *soo* much happier.

Love your lumps and bumps, they are what make you you and what make you real. #RealBeauty!

EXERCISE WISE

#GetMoving

If you are lucky you will love sport and be really good at it. You won't have to think about exercise because you are always on the go. But if you are not, and find exercise a real snore, try some of the Smart Girl ideas below.

Get Personal – just because you don't like sport doesn't mean you don't like exercise. Maybe the whole 'competitive thing' turns you cold. Come up with your own exercise programme and try to do it three times each week.

Get Funky – put on your favourite music and dance around your room. This is great exercise, as it will get your heart pumping in no time.

Get Bendy – yoga is an awesome way to exercise. It helps improve your posture and flexibility, reduces stress and can help you to sleep better. Ask for a DVD for your next Christmas or birthday present or find a class near you.

Get Your Skates On – rollerblading is great exercise, take a pair to the park and get your heart racing.

Get Everybody Moving – you will be much more likely to want to exercise if you enjoy it together as a family. Why not suggest going for a walk together? If you think your family will cramp your style go with a friend. You can have a good goss as you go.

Mirror, Mirror

Do you like what you see when you look in the mirror? If the answer is no, stop right there. TV and adverts can make you believe that there is only one way to look, one definition of beauty. They stop you from seeing how amazing you are. Loving yourself can be hard but making it a priority can make a real difference. Follow these Smart Girl secrets to loving yourself. #NoFilter

You are unique – stop focusing on what you think is wrong with your body and think about all the amazing things it can do. Loving your body will help you to treat it with the respect it deserves.

Be kind to yourself – ever tell yourself that you're a loser, with weird hair and a big chin? If you heard a person talking about someone else that way, you would think they were very mean, so stop talking to yourself that way.

Take five – fight negative feelings by finding at least five things that make you fabulous. #LoveYourself

Be kind to others – do you flick through magazines and say mean things about celebs? Stop! Seeing the positive in others will help you to look for it in yourself. #Don'tBeAHater

Take responsibility – people can tell you that you are pretty, but until you start telling yourself that, you won't hear them. Don't brush off their compliments – be polite and say 'thank you'.

Get comfortable – being confident in your own skin makes other people want to be around you. Love yourself and others will follow.

We all have flaws – even the most beautiful people think they have flaws. The key is to keep it in perspective. If you find yourself feeling unhappy and behaving differently because of how you look, talk to an adult you trust.

The Mushy Stuff

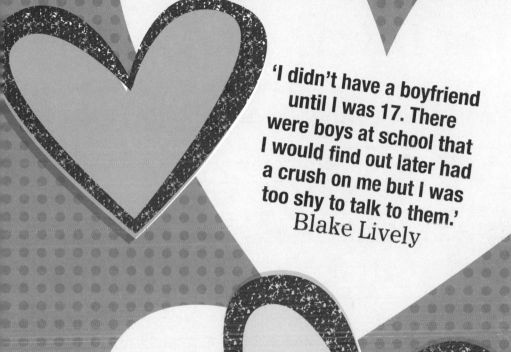

'I didn't have a boyfriend until I was 17. There were boys at school that I would find out later had a crush on me but I was too shy to talk to them.'
Blake Lively

'When I turned 16, I loved boys ... I always loved boys. I still love boys.'
Kate Hudson

Are You Ready for Love?

Are boys all you think about or the last thing on your mind? Take this quiz to find out if you are ready for love.

1. **When you think of your favourite boy in your class, you...**

   a. Want to dance with him.
   b. Want to hold his hand.
   c. Want to tell him a great joke you heard.
   d. Favourite boy? Are you kidding? #SoGross

2. **When your friends talk about boys, you...**

   a. Get ready to share your latest crush. After all, you saw him first!
   b. Shyly wait for your turn to speak.
   c. Wait for everyone to start talking about something else.
   d. Try to change the subject. Boys are *soo* boring.

3. **You hear that a boy in your class likes you. This makes you feel...**

   a. Awesome! It's great to be liked, even if he isn't your dream boy.
   b. Flattered but embarrassed. #WhyIsEverybodyStaring?
   c. Weird. You wish you didn't know

because now you don't know how to act around him.

d. Grossed out. You DO NOT want to talk about it.

4. You are at the school dance and all of the boys are standing on one side of the hall and you and your friends are standing on the other. You...

a. March to the other side of the hall and ask your crush to dance. Someone has to get this party started!

b. Wish someone would come over and ask you to dance.

c. Annoyed – everyone's being so weird.

d. Have a great time! Things are just as they should be.

5. Your best friend has started seeing a boy in your class and wants you to come to the cinema with him and his best friend. You...

a. Jump at the chance. Yay! A real double date!

b. Say yes. He seems nice and it was nice of your friend to think of you.

c. Go along. You haven't spent much time with your friend since she started seeing him.

d. You want no part of it.

MOSTLY As – ahead of the game

You know what you want and don't mind who knows it. Don't be surprised if your confidence sends boys running at first. Boys can be slow to catch on to matters of the heart. Be patient. They are sure to realize your fabulousness soon.

MOSTLY Bs – fluttering your lashes

You like boys, but don't want to shout about it. Maybe there's someone you can't stop thinking about or maybe you just wonder if anyone thinks about you THAT WAY. Why not put yourself out there and talk to a boy you like? He won't bite.

MOSTLY Cs – cool chick

You know boys exist; they are fun, play games and tell jokes, but all this 'my best friend thinks you're nice' and holding-hands stuff is silly. Don't stress, keep being you and one day you might find one boy funnier than the rest.

MOSTLY Ds – enough already

Why is everyone always going on about boys? Boys just turn your friends into boring idiots! Maybe you aren't ready for boys yet but they're not going away anytime soon. Ask your friends if you can talk about something else for a while, otherwise you might have to suck it up or broaden your friendship circle.

Some Smart Girls never get all mushy over boys, in fact some Smart Girls' hearts go all aflutter for other girls. This is known as being lesbian, or gay. Others find themselves falling for boys and girls and this is called being bisexual (or bi). When you are surrounded by a bunch of boy-mad girls, having gay or bisexual feelings can make you feel like a total freak. Take heart, whoever you find yourself crushing on, you ARE NOT a freak and you ARE NOT alone. There are lots of Smart Girls out there who feel the way you do and you WILL meet them, eventually. Anything that makes you feel different at school is really hard, but having gay or bisexual feelings is nothing to be ashamed of, embarrassed about, and is NEVER something to apologize for. Hang in there.

Smart Girl Boy Rules

NEVER ditch your friends for a boy. They were there first and you will really need them if things with the boy don't go to plan.

NEVER do anything that makes you feel awkward or uncomfortable to impress a boy.

REMEMBER boys are people too. Sometimes if you like a boy, you can feel nervous and make jokes about them or tease them. Imagine how you would feel and don't do it.

REMEMBER that your friends might not find your crush as fascinating as you do.

NEVER tease or make jokes about another girl to impress a boy. It does quite the opposite. Feeling nervous is no excuse.

ALWAYS stay safe. Maybe you think you have met your dream boy on a social network. People aren't always what they seem. Make sure you remember the rules for staying safe online (see pages 40–41).

Agony Aunt

Your love tangles unravelled...

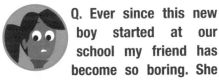

Q. Ever since this new boy started at our school my friend has become so boring. She won't stop talking about him. No matter what we are talking about she always brings it back to him. How can I make her go back to normal?

A. Sounds like your friend has a classic case of 'mentionitis', where even if you are talking about your dog's surgery she compares it to how brave The Boy was when he got a hangnail last week. ARRRGHH! It is totally infuriating. Instead of getting angry, talk to your friend about how you feel. She probably has no idea that she's doing it. You need to understand that this boy is very important to her at the moment. She needs to understand you are very important to her too and that although you are there to listen, you

might need to talk about something else for a bit. Good luck!

Q. I really like this boy in my tennis class but he doesn't seem to know I exist. How can I make him notice me?

A. When you really want someone to notice you, you might think you need to show off, making jokes or being loud. While acting like this will definitely get you noticed, it won't be the real you – just a weird and loud fake you. Try talking to him normally. Ask him what else he likes to do outside of school or how he got such a strong backhand. Not only will this get you talking, but it will also help you get to know him better and find out if you really like him.

Q. I'm so upset. I told my best friend that I really liked this boy in

my class and she went off and told everyone. Now his friends tease me whenever they see me, and he runs away from me. I'm not sure I even like him anymore. Help!

A. The bad news is, you can't do anything to erase this from history. The good news is that eventually, people will forget all about it. Until that happens, use this as an opportunity to show the world how mature you are. When people tease you, don't deny it. Instead use the past tense. Say that you did like him but with all of this drama and with him acting all weird you really aren't so sure any more. Also, have a word with your friend. She really shouldn't have said anything. Maybe she's not the friend to tell your secrets to.

Q. Please help, I think I am in love with this girl in my class. My friend caught me staring at her and told everyone that I am gay and they all started teasing me. Am I gay?

A. I am sorry you're being teased. It isn't fair because it is very likely that some of them have felt the same at some point. Crushing on other girls can feel really intense and make you feel awkward but it's a normal part of growing up. For a lot of girls, these feelings pass and they like boys, but for other girls they don't.

Either way, your feelings are totally natural and you don't have to put up with the teasing. Even if your friends are just trying to be funny, it is upsetting you and it's important that you talk to someone. If you don't know anyone you feel comfortable talking to, call Childline on 0800 1111 or contact the lesbian, gay and bisexual charity Stonewall on 08000 502020. They can give you more information and put you in contact with help in your area.

I can't tell you whether or not you are gay, but I can tell you that if you are, THINGS WILL GET EASIER. At school you can't choose the girls you surround yourself with and let's face it, some of them are far from smart. Everyone is so worried about what other people think that they pick on anyone they see as different. It won't always be that way. As you grow up you will meet other girls who feel like you do, have amazing friends who love you for who you are, and leave the mean girls at school far behind.

Life After School

SCHOOL

'I was glad to leave school. I couldn't relate to kids my own age.' Kristen Stewart

'Really, if I hadn't come home from school miserable every day, maybe I wouldn't have been so motivated to write songs.' Taylor Swift

Dear Future Self...

When things get really tough, try writing a letter to your future self to remind her what you went through.* Imagine who you will be when you are 30, what will you be doing? Who will you be friends with? Where will you work? Where will you live?

Your future self has it easy, right? Well you don't want her to forget how she got there. Take a piece of paper and let her know that she wouldn't be there if it wasn't for the sacrifices you are making right now. What else would you like to say to her?

When you think you have finished, pop your letter in an envelope and seal it. Write your name and the date of your 30th birthday on it and do not open it until then.

*This letter, along with your diary, will make excellent material for your future autobiography. Talk about getting an early start on homework! Well done you!

The Future's Bright...

...the future is yours!

Whether or not your school days suck, wouldn't it be great if every day afterwards didn't? Focusing your mind on the life you want when you leave can really take your mind off even the worst things that happen at school. Good results can help you get the job you want – the fun, interesting job – rather than being stuck with a boring job forever because you didn't like school.

Take a look at the list of dream jobs below. You can start working towards any of these careers right now.

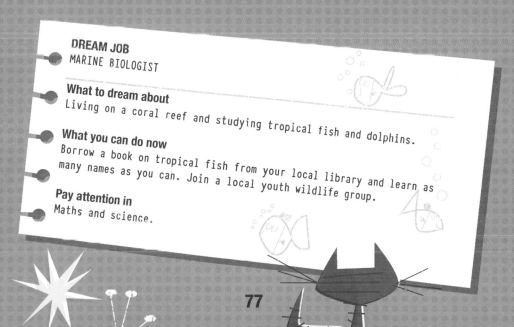

DREAM JOB
MARINE BIOLOGIST

What to dream about
Living on a coral reef and studying tropical fish and dolphins.

What you can do now
Borrow a book on tropical fish from your local library and learn as many names as you can. Join a local youth wildlife group.

Pay attention in
Maths and science.

DREAM JOB
ACTRESS

What to dream about
Playing Juliet at The Globe Theatre, London, or starring in the next hit series on E4.

What you can do now
Audition for as many school performances as you can. Join an after-school theatre club. Practise different emotions in your mirror.

Pay attention in
English, drama, history and all of your subjects. You never know what you may need to draw on for a role.

DREAM JOB
DOCTOR/NURSE

What to dream about
Taking care of people and saving lives at home or anywhere in the world.

What you can do now
Ask your doctor, if there is time at your next appointment, how they became a doctor. Take care of a family member the next time they are ill.

Pay attention in
Maths and science, including physics and chemistry, not just biology.

DREAM JOB
JOURNALIST

What to dream about
Reporting the news from dangerous and exotic places.

What you can do now
Watch the news. Look out for newsworthy stories around you and try to write about them in an exciting way. Join a drama group to give you confidence and a good presenting style. Practise writing daily.

Pay attention in
English, history and all of your subjects. You never know what you will be called to report on.

DREAM JOB
DETECTIVE

What to dream about
Unravelling mysteries and fighting crime.

What you can do now
Do lots of puzzles. Sounds crazy? Tuning your mind to look for patterns and solving the unsolvable will be a good skill in the future.

Pay attention in
All of your subjects. How else will you be able to take down a criminal mastermind?

DREAM JOB
WRITER

What to dream about
Writing stories to be enjoyed by readers all over the world from anywhere in the world!

What you can do now
Start writing now, even if it is just a diary. Write every day.

Pay attention in
English – and all of your subjects. The heroine of one of your novels could be a great scientist. Being a great writer means knowing a little about everything.

DREAM JOB
BANKER OR TOP EXECUTIVE

What to dream about
Buying and selling shares, making big business decisions and making millions.

What you can do now
Start watching the news and reading the financial pages in the newspaper.

Pay attention in
Maths and science.

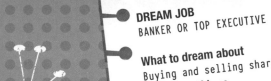

DREAM JOB
CHEF

What to dream about
Running your own kitchen, having your own TV show and making delicious food.

What you can do now
Ask your parents to teach you how to make their favourite recipes and experiment in the kitchen. Borrow cookbooks from the library.

Pay attention in
Science – believe it or not, great cooking is a science. Learning as much as you can about what happens to things when you mix them together and heat them will really help you in the kitchen.

DREAM JOB
FASHION DESIGNER

What to dream about
Creating your own collections of fabulous clothes.

What you can do now
Ask your parents if you can have a go at making a simple skirt from a pattern. Experiment with different outfits from your own wardrobe.

Pay attention in
Art, design and technology and history – lots of designers get their inspiration from the past.

DREAM JOB
VET

What to dream about
Saving the lives of kittens and puppies - cute!

What you can do now
Borrow books about all of your favourite animals from your local library. Ask your parents if you can have a pet. Enquire at your local vet or animal shelter if they have a work experience programme.

Pay attention in
Maths and science - you need top marks to become a vet.

DREAM JOB
HAIR STYLIST

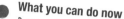

What to dream about
Having your own top salon and creating super-cool hairstyles.

What you can do now
Practise styling your own and your friends' hair - without scissors! Cut styles you like out of your magazines. Look at styles from the past in history books at the library.

Pay attention in
Art, maths and science - having a good knowledge of maths will help you run your own business and science could really help out when it comes to formulating your own line of styling products.

Motivate Yourself

Sometimes getting yourself through your homework and revision can be a real slog, but getting what you want doesn't happen by chance. It takes hard work and dedication. Keep yourself motivated through even the dullest projects by making your own motivational poster.

1. Cut out pictures from magazines of women that inspire you.

2. Print out pictures from the Internet of people and things that motivate you – make sure to ask your parents before using up all of the paper.

3. Cut out pictures of homes, clothes and cars you would like to have and places you'd love to visit when you are a grown-up.

4. Write down inspirational quotes from famous people or good comments teachers have given you to keep you inspired.

> 'Nothing is impossible, the word itself says "I'm possible"!'
> – Audrey Hepburn

5. Glue all of your pictures to a piece of card and keep it somewhere near to where you do your homework or pin them to a board above your desk.

6. Look at it whenever you are finding things hard and want to give up.

Don't worry if you change your mind about what you want to do, it's just paper, simply recycle it and start again!

'No matter who you are, no matter what you did, no matter where you've come from, you can always change, become a better version of yourself.' – Madonna

'You will face many defeats in your life, but never let yourself be defeated.' – Maya Angelou

'Always have a vivid imagination, for you never know when you might need it.' – J.K. Rowling

Real Smart Girls

Check out these real-life Smart Girls. Living proof that you can become whoever you want to be, no matter who you are and where you come from.

Oprah Winfrey
Born: 1954

Then: As a girl, Oprah was so poor that she had to wear dresses made from old flour sacks. As she grew up Oprah suffered abuse and faced bullying, racism and sexism. She worked hard and did well in school even though she had a very difficult home life. When she was 17, Oprah won a beauty pageant sponsored by a radio station that gave her a part-time job presenting the news.

Now: For 25 years Oprah presented her very own mega-successful TV show, and became the world's first black, female billionaire. She owns her own TV channel, publishes her own magazine, founded a school for underprivileged girls in South Africa and donates millions of dollars to charities. She has even been nominated for an Oscar!

Quotes: 'The biggest adventure you can take is to live the life of your dreams.'

'I don't think of myself as a poor deprived ghetto girl who made good. I think of myself as somebody who from an early age knew I was responsible for myself, and I had to make good.'

Malala Yousafzai
Born: 1997

Then: Malala grew up in Pakistan. She spoke out and blogged on international news websites about girls' rights to education after girls in her area were banned from attending school. She overcame persecution for speaking out and survived being shot by the Taliban.

Now: Malala lives in England and was nominated for the 2013 Nobel Peace Prize. She has published her own bestselling autobiography and speaks at conventions and to politicians all over the world, including at the United Nations.

Quotes: 'I raise up my voice – not so I can shout but so that those without a voice can be heard… We cannot succeed when half of us are held back.'

'Let us pick up our books and our pens, they are the most powerful weapons.'

Emma Watson
Born: 1990

Then: Grew up while starring in the mega-successful *Harry Potter* films and yet still managed to fit her schoolwork around filming and modelling. She achieved excellent grades in all of her exams. #WayToGoHermione!

Now: As well as studying at Brown University, Rhode Island USA, she continues to act in successful Hollywood films.

Quotes: 'I want to be a Renaissance woman. I want to paint, I want to write, I want to act. I just want to do everything.'

'I've always given 100 per cent. I can't do it any other way.'

Jessica Ennis
Born: 1986

Then: Jessica was the smallest in her class and was bullied by the bigger girls. She used to dread going to school and dreaded it even more when the same bullies followed her to secondary school. Instead of fighting, Jessica confided in her diary and eventually her mum. Her mum signed her up to an out-of-school sports camp where she began to compete.

Now: An Olympic gold-medal-winning athlete with numerous sponsorship deals, Jessica Ennis was the face of the 2012 London Olympic Games and is an inspiration to women all over the world.

Quotes: 'I have been called many things, from tadpole to poster girl, but I have had to fight to make that progression.'

'It is an age where young people are fed ideas of quick-fix fame and instant celebrity, but the tears mean more if the journey is hard. So I don't cry crocodile tears; I cry the real stuff.'

Sheryl Sandberg
Born: 1969

Then: At school, Sheryl was top of her class and considered a serious geek. She went on to graduate from one of the top colleges in America and worked at the White House. After a career break, Sheryl took the brave step of becoming Vice President at what was then a new company, Google.

Now: Sheryl is now the COO (Chief Operating Officer) of Facebook and has written an internationally bestselling guidebook for women on succeeding in business, *Lean In*.

Quotes: 'I want to tell any young girl out there who's a geek, I was a really serious geek in high school. It works out. Study harder.'

'Until women are as ambitious as men, they're not going to achieve as much as men.'

'All the things that make you uncool in high school, are the things that are good for your life.'

It's a Girl's World

Well not quite yet, but it's getting there. There's still a lot to do, but with a Smart Girl like you on the case it will be a girl's world in no time.

Are you a feminist?

Answer these two questions to find out.

1. **Your brother gets 50p a week more pocket money than you, because he is a boy. Do you think this is:**

   a. Fair
   b. Unfair

2. **You are working on a group project to build a robot. The boys have decided that they are in charge of building and you will write it up because you are a girl and have pretty handwriting and know nothing about robots. Do you think this is:**

   a. Fair
   b. Unfair

Conclusion

Both **B**, surely? #LikeDuh!
CONGRATULATIONS! You are a feminist, like millions of brave, brilliant and inspiring women and men that came before you.

1. Giving your brother more money, just because he's a boy. That can't happen right? Wrong. It happens every single day. In the UK, women earn 15 per cent less than their male colleagues doing the same jobs. Fifteen per cent is the equivalent of a woman working for over a month each year for free while her male colleague is getting paid. #Ridiculous

2. So what if you have pretty handwriting? (Don't worry if you don't, lots of very Smart Girls have dreadful handwriting.) Being

excluded, just because you are a girl, is totally out of order. There are thousands of female engineers, mathematicians, physicists, astronauts, pilots and soldiers. There may not be as many women as men in these roles but with more and more Smart Girls, like you, standing up for themselves, the gap is closing. #Let'sDoThis!

F is for fairness

Feminism is something people can get very shouty about, for good reason, but all that shouting can scare a girl off and make her not want to call herself a feminist. Don't fall into that trap.

Being a feminist means caring about and standing up for fairness, and believing that someone shouldn't be excluded, judged, abused, exploited or ignored just because she is female.

Feminist myths #Busted!

You can like pink and be a feminist.
You can like boys and be a feminist.
You can like kittens and be a feminist.
You can like fashion and be a feminist.
You can like ballet and be a feminist.
You can like dolls and be a feminist.
You can want to look pretty and be a feminist.

Smart Girl, stand up!

Feminists of the past have done incredible things and we have so much to thank them for, but there is still a lot to do. All over the world, girls and women are excluded from education, voting, driving cars and wearing what they like. They live in fear of persecution and violence. The only way to guarantee that this won't change is to say nothing – so take a stand and speak up.

The Smart Money is on You

Whether you only have a few pounds in your piggy bank or thousands tucked away in savings, the one thing you can guarantee about money is that you will always want a bit more. Read on to discover how to make your money go far.

Resist the impulse

If you are just going into town with your parents, or to the park, leave your purse at home. This will stop you wasting money on stuff you don't need. If you see something you want, you can come back and buy it later if you decide you definitely want it, rather than impulse buying and regretting it.

Keep a diary

Ever wonder where your money goes? Keep a record of every penny you spend. Do this for a couple of weeks and then take a look. Wow, did you really need to spend all that on stickers and flapjacks?! Ugh.

Save

This may sound boring, but saving is not only sensible, it actually makes future fun possible. If you are lucky enough to get some money for your next birthday or Christmas, put it in a bank account. Keep adding to it when you can, and watch your money grow.

Don't be afraid of it

When you are afraid of something, it is really tempting to bury your head in the sand and ignore it. This is how you end up having spent all of your pocket money the day after you got it … AGAIN!! Face your fears. Make a point to always know how much money you have. Getting into good habits now will make your life much easier.

Think about the future

Maybe you are 100 per cent sure of what you want to do with your life and money isn't going to make any difference. If you haven't decided yet, why not do some research on the Internet and at the library to see if you can find out how much people earn in careers you might want to pursue. Lots of jobs may sound really boring, but when you realize that 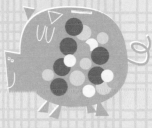 you can earn a fortune doing them, they might not seem so bad. You are going to spend a lot of your life at work, you may as well get paid well for it.

Money is not a dirty word

Wanting to be secure and have enough money to be able to have the kind of life you want is smart, but that's not everything. Money can make a difference, too. Bill Gates, founder of Microsoft, and one of the richest men on the planet has personally donated nearly $30 billion to his charitable foundation. He can probably still afford to buy as many new outfits and magazines as he wants, too.

Real-Life Cringes

Feel for your Smart Girl sisters and learn from what they did when embarrassment struck. See I told you, even the most embarrassing thing can become a funny story one day.

The Escalator of Terror

'My maxi skirt got caught in an escalator in the middle of the shopping centre on a busy Saturday. They had to stop the escalator with everyone on it and I had to step out of my skirt. I was standing there in just my coat and knickers. I had to laugh when my friend wrapped her coat around my legs and said, "Thank goodness you're alive! You could have been fashion's first victim!" We still laugh about it.'

Leah, aged 10

Rolling into Ruin

'Our school had an inset day so I decided to go roller skating up the street with my friends. There was a school up my street that didn't have an inset day. All the kids were in the playground and my friends and I decided to skate past to show off that we were off school and they weren't. As we were skating by, I stuck out my tongue but then tripped on the curb and fell over. It felt like the whole school was laughing. My friends found it pretty funny, too. I'm over it now, but I still cross the road whenever I walk past in case anyone recognizes me.'

Cally, aged 11

Surfs Up, Pants Down!

'I wore my new bikini to the beach with my friends. We were all body boarding in the waves when I got swept up in a big one and was churned up in the surf. The wave carried me right onto the shore WITHOUT MY BIKINI BOTTOMS! I had to cover myself with seaweed and run to our towels to change. Now I ALWAYS wear a one piece for surfing. I never did find my bikini bottoms, LOL.'

Louise, aged 10

Goodbye and Good Luck

Still there, Smart Girl? Yay! You made it to the end. Nice work!

Well, what did you think? Helpful? Funny? Totally pointless? Fingers crossed you found something in here you can use.

No book in the world can stop bad things from happening to you or prevent your trousers coming down in public (this actually happened to me, more than once). What a book can do is help you to handle whatever life throws at you and remind you that how you feel right now, no matter how sad or happy, is not how you are going to feel forever. Even the worst feelings will pass and what you need to do, through all of it, is to Stay Smart and Carry On!

Goodbye and good luck,

Sally xxx